# A JOURNEY UNTO PEACE

## Dr Phil Stack

# A JOURNEY UNTO PEACE

**How much** good is required for peace to exist? And how many persons arc needed who will give more and sacrifice more and receive less to sustain peace? How much good in giving is required when giving is offered to accommodate many needs? And forgiving? How many are willing to forgive? And how many will have sufficient goodness to be caring, listening to others, and to be understanding and accepting of others?

**The time has come,**

**A JOURNEY UNTO PEACE.**

I invited five, a Presbyterian, a Lutheran and a Catholic, all pastors. And there were two more, a female teacher and myself, a Psychologist.

The five were seated in the rectory of St Wenceslaus Church on a cold wintry afternoon as beautiful chimes of some unseen timepiece enchanted the adventurers.

# A JOURNEY UNTO PEACE

What was the plan? We were coming together without an agenda. Just to be.

The female member of the group was first to speak: "I constantly have to smile at myself since a long time ago, and in many places where I find myself, I find men saying to me, "you do a good job for a woman."

It took me a long time to overcome that, having become a little bitchy in the process. Fortunately, I am mature enough now to know who I am and what I want to do, and it really doesn't matter what they think of me. 1 think others have great difficulty in being accepted and being loved in their meanderings through life. I sometimes have difficulty with people who precede me, who achieve a status before I get there. They attach a label on me, "A minister's wife." It is as if I must wait until they are able to see me as a person, without labels."

"We love you because you are a special person," someone said.

"I'm a good teacher, but not a scholar. If I should count my talents..."

"You have many, many talents," the voice of one of the men interrupted,

"Many, many," another concurred.

"Actually, the label doesn't bother me as it once did. If you say, 'you arc Ron's wife,' I accept that. I don't consider being married to a profession or a house. Such pigeon-holing used to bother me. but my husband had the guts to let me be me."

"Well, you are a very valuable person; you are the best, right now."

# A JOURNEY UNTO PEACE

*(The disclosures between members of the group continued)*

"I've been blessed by knowing people whom I call 'great,' people who have helped touch my life and enabled me to unfold. Helping someone else is one of the great things we can do in this life. We've all experienced people. Without them I would hesitate to think where would we be now. I'm sure this is true with you also, Dave."

"Whenever I needed somebody in life, there was always somebody, and many times that somebody had never known it. We never know what lives we touch."

"I know the things in life that continually stirred me pertain to reaching out to others."

"Just as you are, it's good enough. Your life is as mine has been for me, receiving from fine people. It is like a whole new creation."

"The same with me. Many beautiful experiences for me have come from people and, hopefully, I'll be able to give as beautifully as they."

"1 think I feel I'm venturing on my own now. I don't have to worry about others, what they think of me or what they expect. I am just assured that whatever I do, I do the best I can."

"Whatever I give to any of you, it is yours. You are deserving of it."

"I don't know how I can pay you back."

"Repayment is unnecessary; it's just for you. That's how it is."

"It's kind of a nice world we live in."

"Uh.huh."

"Our payback, if there is any such thing, is making this available to others."

# A JOURNEY UNTO PEACE

"It is in receiving that we give."

"**What must** there be in a person's background that enables him to be a giving person?"

"That probably is unimportant. A person who can give, gives."

"You are a tremendous giver. I know because you give much."

"I guess I need to give. It is just as natural as life itself. If I don't have takers I must search for them."

"You never deplete those."

"What would happen in a society of all givers?"

"It seems you must have givers and takers simultaneously for the effective functioning of our imperfect state."

"Well, occasionally we must all take."

"Probably, if you were to arrange a formula for giving, it would include the opposite of what we ordinarily adhere to, and that is the concept of the wonderful, magnificent, beautiful quality of "selfishness". I think, if one is aware of his selfishness, then he is in a much better position to distinguish between his selfless actions and his selfish actions. When he knows what his selfish actions are then he doesn't need to hide them."

"We subscribe to the concept of "helping," a Christian involvement, more in keeping with how we relate to others in society. But is "helping" more inferior than is "giving?""

"With helping one is obligated at intervals. When a helping need arises for someone, then you feel the urgency of rescue. With "giving," however there is a continuous commitment, a constant focus, a sense of searching for need in others. By giving we have looked inwardly. Thus we are continuously alerted to what we are, what we are becoming.

When we help we feel ourselves being unselfish....so helping proves we can express our unselfishness. On the other hand, with giving, we do not have to prove our unselfishness.

If we do things in life without needing to prove something, then we are better off for it. With helping we know we are doing for others; with giving we know how to do better."

"That's beautiful."

"That is good. In helping we wait until the situation arises; in giving we head off the worsening of the condition. 'That's good."

"Giving is a prevention because it acts on lives continuously, not only in emergency situations."

"It's really a new thought, idealizing selfishness."

"It's sort of heretical."

"Yeah!"

"It's comforting and reassuring, though."

"Just be yourself"

"To know what we are."

"It's hard to accept this matter of selfishness."

"Yeah, it's such a drastic change of mentality from what we've known."

**All my life** I was afraid of some kind of judgment. As a little girl a minister told me if I did something wrong, I would be put in the dark with a tarantula."

"A what?"

"A tarantula, furry legs and everything. Yes a real live one that's crawling around in the dark."

"Ai-yi-yi!"

"That's really putting the fear of the Lord in you."

"I was a pre-teener too; before I was ten years old."

"The fear of hell, right from Hades."

"That's what I call a bell-ringer. It rang a bell in my head that said, 'it can't be possible; it just can't be true."

"How about the poor kid who would gobble that up?"

"How could such a terrible thing be done in the name of God?"

"Yeah, 1 was just thinking the same thing."

"Why, why in that field when you can't get away with this kind of approach in any other profession."

"It's a matter of their being loving people. When I reached the point of needing for myself, there were more love-giving people who gave. As for the church, there surely are abundant changes that it needs in
this age. Yet I cannot imagine an age without the church because of every single person who has been profoundly influenced in his life has been through a faith of some kind."

"I guess we can't be that pessimistic."

"I don't think we can."

**"I have some** apples for you."

"Thank you very much, Greg."

"Thank you."

"Thank You."

"Compliments of Dave's refrigerator."

"What is mine is yours."

"Just think what would happen if man were free to do as he pleases and nothing would inhibit his conduct"

"What kind of chaos would you have us living in?"

"I see it as an opportunity for freedom."

"But what do you mean by "freedom?" What do I need to be free to do what I now do not do?"

"I'm thinking of freedom in a good sense. It would be freedom from inhibiting factors, guilty feelings especially. Freedom to be yourself, acknowledging one's worth; the freedom to handle oneself.

Give man acceptance and see by what leaps and bounds he will grow."

"I guess it's like a freedom to know yourself without being afraid of what you will find. A freedom to distinguish between that part of yourself you have hidden for years and that part you have felt free to show to other people. It would be a kind of realization of yourself totally."

"I think there is probably freedom in having a choice between a selfish act and selfless act. As I go and grab these apples, I think of you people and say, "they would like to have one.' Here I am in a position of exercising freedom. I can take one for myself alone and leave you out of it. I know that is part of me also. Then I have the freedom of making a distinction. But I am unable to make that distinction unless I know that part of me and this part of me. So, being aware of my selfishness, I can make the determination to be selfless.

Another individual can go through his whole life being unselfish and may I not do this minute thing, still being unselfish but not being aware of that other part of himself So there is more value in freedom when we can decide between selfish and unselfish actions applicable to the self than there is in making the distinction between right and wrong, which are externally imposed categories."

"It is far more meaningful when one is given the dignity of making a distinction regarding one's actions. There is more freedom in it because one is allowed that freedom.

"I get the feeling you are saying, in order for a man to be free, he must have a sense of worth. He must have a sense of value to be free. This kind of freedom immediately implies responsibility to self, not to an external influence."

"That's correct. We cannot possibly feel a feeling of worth and not show it. As you have the feeling of self-worth then others are influenced by your feeling of that worth. You become more priceless to me as the value I have for myself increases. Then your value also increases. In this vital way man needs man.

"So, as you help me increase my value, your value also increases. To venture forth and treat others with value is a relatively simple process. You've done it with an ordinary compliment."

"It's relatively simple, but we see so little of it being done."

"It is difficult to give value to another if we seek the same for ourselves."

That will change."

"Very Good."

"It's changing now."

*(A pall of peacefulness descends on the group as the relishing of silence increases. A basket is being passed around. Each apple core produces a thud as it strikes the bottom of the empty container. The usual "Thank You" followed in precision with one exception.)*

**I didn't thank** him for offering the basket because I felt I deserved it from him."

"You did deserve it."

"Indeed you did"

"If 1 say 'thank you' it's like saying, maybe I don't deserved it. It would be like giving something back in return. Our objective is to avoid the repayment."

"I don't have to give him anything: he doesn't have to give me anything, but we both may decide to give to each other without expecting a payback."

"The more value you give to a person, the less you will expect repayment."

"In the context of this small family of ours, this would be totally acceptable, but in other, larger societies, it would not be desirable."

"I think the statement is very valid, but it is such a biting indictment of the word "Love." Love means you never have to say 'I'm

Sorry.' A lot of people couldn't grasp that concept."

"By golly, that statement is worth the whole journey. I can chew on that for a week."

"I'm so glad that you are with me here. You don't have to require any reason for your presence."

"Well, I must treat you differently because I value you very highly."

*(The chimes were chiming six o'clock; five o'clock passed unnoticed. Some shoes were off. Tensions were gone. The room grew heavily laden with the comfort of unity as silence crept into every crevice of the room.)*

**"Is silence an** indication that we don't have to prove anything?

"I'm very comfortable."

"It's comfortable here too. How is the climate for the others?"

"It's just blossoming."

"It's rather quiet now."

"Tranquil."

"It is like the wind whispering through the pines."

"It is peaceful. Do we encounter many peaceful moments like this during an average week or month?"

"Only when you meet people of like feeling."

"It is peaceful enough to be unique. It is harmonious."

"I feel so."

"For this transition it requires people of like minds to provide the spirit. I am reflecting on coming to myself."

# A JOURNEY UNTO PEACE

"How can you experience this uniqueness? We don't have to pretend. I couldn't have discovered this peace by myself."

"Contemplation is a perfect union with God. Passing through different stages we finally come to the most ideal, the contemplative. I feel we have it now. We are bound by our togetherness."

*(The nurturing silence holds fast to the small band of people, as if it would last forever. It was 8:00 o'clock and nobody was noticing.)*

**I think a** perfect society would be worthless unless there is a new way for people to communicate."

"We surly cover a great deal with words."

"Maybe we discovered something."

"Maybe I talk too much."

"You deserve all the peace of the moment we can give you."

"Your thoughts are exquisite."

"I wonder, in a sense, if this is the climax, the objective for man to strive for. It has come to the point where we don't have to say anything."

"We are really together, we feel together."

"Somehow, through talking, we reached this silent stage."

"Might we not soak it up, then do another talking binge to reach another stage?"

"Maybe we found it."

"That's too easy. I'm not ready to have found it"

"Oh, it will come. At least we have found it or it will come."

'The words that we will express after this period will assume different meaning."

*(A thick, hard silence lays, unmoving in the room)*

**"I wonder what** our awareness of time is now?"

"Who cares. I placed time on a back shelf for awhile."

"Me too."

"I'm so enjoying this, time can wait."

"Can we verbalize what this experience means to us?" It is a kind of unification of sorts. The fact of our putting time on our shelf may be a sign of our harmony with the universe, which is timeless."

"Yeah, it feels like time never runs out. It is eternal."

"It is a taste of eternity."

"Is this timeless state something we strive for in life?"

"Is this our objective, the condition of timelessness, of unification, of harmony and peacefulness."

"Yes. I like the word 'harmony."

"How did we achieve this harmony in this short span of time? We all feel it; it is just as real as anything. Could it come about individually? If we were not all present, could we still have it?"

"No. We needed each other's help. We needed each other's assurance of our worth and value. We needed acceptance. To me this brings about a harmonious feeling within ourselves and with others. By myself I could not feel unique unless I found it coming from someone."

"Is this the result of some balance between giving and receiving?"

"We have received and we have given."

"I think so. The initiative is through God who gives through others. We first receive, then we can give. The initiative belongs to someone else. Maybe some take that to mean, on their own, man cannot merit anything, or is helpless?"

"Man is capable. To me this is realistic, though, by myself, I could never make this discovery."

"So this giving and taking might contribute to our present state. In a sense, it is a leveling of the mountains and a making of the crooked ways straight."

"Making the ways straight ...this is symbolic...and having made the ways straight, we will continue ahead more surely."

"St John the Baptist made the way for Christ who was the coming of peace....it's like making the way straight so that peace can come to us."

"But the way is made straight by the give and take process. All of us here, we have giving and taking properties. Among us here, there is always somebody who is available to give. This is a very secure feeling. Regardless of what pained situation we bring up we have the reassurance that somebody will take care of it."

"It seems that harmony is the balance between giving and taking in every man's life. Even as he is a perfect giver, he is also a good receiver, and I guess we need an even mixture of both. That creates a harmonious feeling in ourselves and in others."

"We are as a rock receiving the heat of the hot sun during the day. Being thoroughly filled up with warmth, the rock then gives the heat to the chilly night. Having received warmth, it can now give warmth."

"But we have this experience all at once, all together. Somehow we are affected by each other."

"I'm sure of it. I am affected by the peace I see in others."

"How can a person be at peace with himself when he sees others who are clearly not at peace with themselves."

"As we go our separate ways we will carry that peaceful quality to others. By seeing our peacefulness, they may also be peaceful."

"If we want others to be a certain way, we must be that way ourselves."

"We are the examples of what others will be. It is not telling a person what to do, it is being an example for him."

"One of the beauties of this afternoon has been this unstructured situation. We have come here without preparation, with no agenda, armed with our giving and taking attributes. Perhaps we found that we had a natural proclivity to seek. Even with the outside regimen we may continue our peacefulness and, hopefully, share the process with others who are searching."

"So, it is inevitable that we are here, present, in this state. We may see ourselves as being here for this or that reason, but this state of harmony was inevitable."

# A JOURNEY UNTO PEACE

"That was a beautiful thought. Perhaps if we became defenseless others will become like us, less defensive."

"We have come from a society that we all know, and we have somehow entered God's universe."

"This is the ultimate, the timelessness of the peace of heaven is like this, think we have come closest to it. But this is what all men strive for. It is a harmony with man's humanity to man and with God's universe."

"This is like prayer."

**"This is like** a total fearlessness. We have no fear of each other and realize the positive, unexpressed assurance that all is well."

"It is peace, music, a choir somewhere singing, a real organ playing, and yet. There is no music . It is quiet."

"It is like a God of silence. He doesn't have to say anything."

"It is a stilled, small voice. God isn't in the thunder; He isn't in the lightning ...just a stilled small voice."

"It's as if we allowed our own individual identities to become fused into one greater, unified identity."

"Perhaps death is as peaceful as this."

"It is almost like a total giving and a total taking simultaneously."

"That is the definition of death. It is a total giving of life and a total taking of God's love."

"A final moment of complete release."

# A JOURNEY UNTO PEACE

"It is a religious experience tuning into that which is beyond."

"I have a sense of assurance that I have received something that I cherish deeply, This has been a far beyond good experience for me." It has a sense of the eternal. You care and I care and, adding this together, makes it nothing short of magnificent."

"To me it is like a great mind expander, like drugs. What people seek through drugs we are finding through each other."

"Might you say that the taking of drugs as a release, escape, or mind expander may represent a searching for concordance with people?"

"I am not using my intellect in this process. That would take labor."

"This is more bliss."

"It is almost as if we touched it would be warm and supportive."

"But we are touching. It is an act of communion."

"This is where man needs to move, in the direction of this kind of peacefulness. If you have peace within, then how can you war against someone? It is impossible; so our objective is to forever have this peace that we may offer it to others."

"I'm mostly aware of the feeling of contentedness. It's a purring, kind of restful feeling, a feeling that all is well. There are no troubles, no anxieties, no worries."

"But is this an unrealistic feeling?"

"Is it not reality to realize that your problems are not as great as they used to be?"

# A JOURNEY UNTO PEACE

"We are better prepared to go out to the highways and byways to serve man."

"Except for the problems, all things are peaceful. If man is peaceful, then the problem is peaceful."

"Is this a state of something-ness or nothing-ness?"

"There is something here."

"There is a lot here. There is lot to live for."

"One thing that would be farthest from the mind would be suicide. There is so much in life for us."

"The purpose of that light on the table there is to give light and, yet, we were down on the floor, out of the way. We have been lifted up, the table put under us, so now we are the light."

# A JOURNEY UNTO PEACE

"I feel an undergirding, an under-support, which will help me fulfill the purpose of better living."

"We are like little hammers, forged into a big hammer. The bigger hammer has the greater strength. As little hammers we derive strength from the bigger hammer. We have a bigger brother now. He is going to fight our battles."

"That sounds good. He's like God. God is peaceful. He is at rest. I think that's what the strength is...and we are showing that kind of strength."

"The value of God through man has, perhaps more merit, than the value of God through religion."

"Amen."

"Because the other you have always had, and it doesn't compare."

"Uh, huh."

"It's the study of strength."

"I'm being fascinated by that word. You know there is strength in this sort of climate. God created the world and the 7th day He rested, and all was finished. Just to be present is enough to reflect on our being, as we are made, is not having to prove ourselves anymore."

"Is this what life is, a constant struggle to prove ourselves?

"Sometimes I feel it for myself. I see myself going frantically from one thing to another."

"Are we all searching for this, A respite? Are we hoping that every day will be like this day or, at least, to have in every day the wonderful feelings of this day."

"It just struck me: if we are communicating through ourselves, through our spirit, then we won't need other activities to build other people up because, there being with us will be enough. God doesn't have to do anything anymore because He is just what He is."

"Maybe the words of the scriptures can become more enlightening when God says: "I AM WHAT AM." No further proof is needed."

*(Eleven chimes rang out slowly, the eleventh hour being like the first)*

## CONCLUSION

Five came to be together one afternoon for no particular reason and achieved a beautiful harmony of togetherness and simultaneous peace within.

They discovered the timeless-ness and peacefulness of "heaven" which significantly distracted them from the cares of the world. With the noble attributes of forgiveness and giving by assuring each other of their value and worth, members were able to feel loved unconditionally. The group became a powerfully protective force for good for each member.

Eventually silence became so pervasive that words became unnecessary and intrusive.

Each of the group members felt they had something important to share with the world.

Eventually the group dispersed and each went separate ways, energized to serve the Lord.

**Dr Phil Stack**
Pstackups@yahoo.com
3343 Taylorwood Ln
Spring Hill, TN 37174

THANK GOD FOR THE
GOOD YOU SAY,
AND FOR THE GOOD YOU
DO;
IT IS A FAR BETTER
WORLD
JUST BECAUSE OF
YOU

LET ME DO WHAT I
CAN
FOR WHOMEVER I CAN
WITH WHAT I HAVE
AND WHERE I AM

# A JOURNEY UNTO PEACE

## ABOUT THE AUTHOR

Dr Philip Stack is a Pennsylvanian by birth and son of refugee parents. He is currently a resident of Spring Hill, Tennessee.

As a Clinical Psychologist he considers the happy, intact family a crucial part of a healthy society. He and his wife are parents of one girl and five boys. They have twenty grand children and are married 57 years.

Dr Stack has practiced in several mental health facilities over a period of 35 years. About his book "How To Do Family Therapy" Hans Selye writes: "Let me congratulate you upon having written a fine and enlightening work." Dr stack identifies The Love Force as a primary agent in healing the malfunctioning family group. The Love Force exists everywhere in nature and it's healing power may be transmitted mainly from one person to another.

Dr Stack identities the improvement in family relationships as "change through no change." Psychological needs are identified and accommodated. Offering acceptance, reassurance and understanding is an effective and necessary requirement.

In his philosophy, Dr Stack offers a simple guideline: "Give the therapeutic power of your compliments generously to the world that the Love Force may enter people's lives and allow peace and happiness to flourish.

Dr Stack is author of "How To Be Good," "Hail to the Second Best," "Secrets of a Romantic Man," and "How we raised our children to serve the Lord."

# A JOURNEY UNTO PEACE

*Unconditional Love:*

*Know that you are born to be*

*Loved Forever*

*Let me do what I can*

*For whomever I can*

*With what I have*

*And where I am.*

*By Dr. Phil Stack and Fe'*

*Servants to the Lord*

"*Thank God for the good you say*

*and for the good you do;*

*It is a far better world*

*Just because of*

*YOU*"

# A JOURNEY UNTO PEACE

## Other Books by Dr. Phil Stack

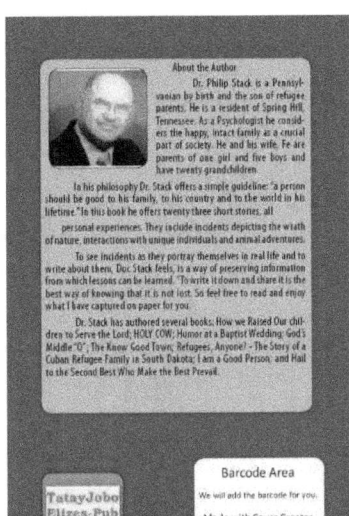

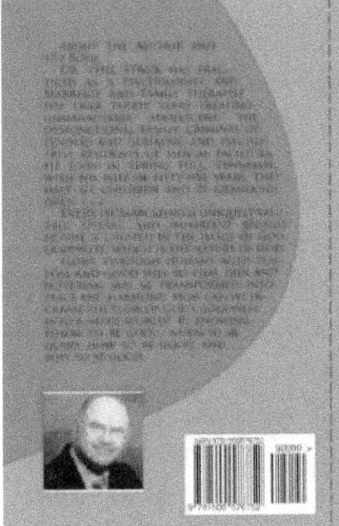

# A JOURNEY UNTO PEACE

**Self-published & printed in USA by Tatay Jobo Elizes** with Author's permission using Print-On-Demand System (POD) and Kindle Edition. Tatay Jobo Elizes is a Self-Publisher in USA. Published in 2015 under the following ISBN numbers.

**ISBN-13:** 978 – 1508931386

**ISBN-10:** 1508931380

# A JOURNEY UNTO PEACE

*--oo--*

Book List - Buy online as paperback or kindle,
Contact: job_elizes@yahoo.com, tatay@usa.com
Websites: http://tinyurl.com/mj76ccq +
www.jobelizes.webs.com

**Writings 1 Book, 2012** , Articles by **Bambi Harper +
Butch Jiimenez + Dr. Phil Stack + Noel Alegre + Toto
Causing +_ Melanie Ferrer + Susie Barbieri _ Rodel
Ramos + Sylvia Salvador + Tatay Jobo Elizes + +
Writings 2 Book, 2012, Artices by Gov. Grace Padaca
+ Melanie Aquino + Toto Causing + Rodel Rodis +
Cesar Torres + Joey Concepcion + Charity Guides +
Cesar Lumba +_ Casiano Mayor Jr. + Sonny Coloma +
Anonymous.+ +**

**Writings 3A Book, 2012**, Articles by **Norman Madrid +
Dr. Rene Azurin + Ernie Delfin + Toto Causing + Dr.
Jose Abueva + MarVic Cagurangan + Casiano Mayor
Jr + Rod Garcia + Roy Gaane + Tatay Jobo Elizes + +
Writings 3B Book, 2012**, Articles by **Ceres Busa +
John Reyes + Bert Guiang. + + Writings 4A Book,
2012**, Articles by **Dr Jose Abueva + Col. Dennis Acop
+ Fred Natividad + Irineo P. Goce, KaPule2 + Miguel
Reynadlo + Marjorie Ann Elizes Reyes+ + Writings 4B
Book, 2012**, 1. Mi Ultimo Adios (My Last Farewell), *Dr.
Jose P. Rizal* + 2. Aling Pagibig Sa Tinubuang
Bayan, *Gat. Andres Bonifacio* + Articles by **Irineo P.
Goce or KaPule2 + +**

**Writings 5 Book - "Best Hopes" 2010** (About
President P-Noy), Articles by **Tony Meloto +
F.SionilJose + Juan L. Mercado + OFWs Letter +
Marcelo Tecson + Cesar Torres+ Perry Diaz + Dr.**

# A JOURNEY UNTO PEACE

Philip S. Chua + Ernie Delfin + Atty. Ted Laguatan + Frank Wenceslao Jaileen F. Jimeno + Tatay Jobo Elizes + + **Writings 6 Book, 2010** + I. SONA - State Of Nation Address - English - *Pres. Benigno Aquino III* + II. SONA - State of Nation Address - Pilipino - *Pres. Benigno Aquino III* + III. First 100 Days peech - Pilipino - *Pres. Benigno Aquino III* + *Artiucles by Bert Guiang* + *Tony Meloto* + *Felicito or Tong C. Payumo* + *Cesar Lumba* + *Flor Lacanilao* + *Juan DelaCruz or Txtmanika* + *Dr. Ramon Marquez* + *Joey Jamito* + *Percival Cruz* + *Rod Garcia* + *Orion Perez Dumdum* + *Sarah Raymundo.* + +

**Writings 7 Book,** 2010 - My Vintage Pics - Pictorials & Family, Tatay Jobo Elizes + + **Writings 8 Book, 2010,** Articles by Gel Santos Relos + Ms.Mike Portes + Jose Ma. Montelibano + Tony Meloto + Dr. Philip S. Chua + Dr. Cesar D. Candari + Dr. Eliseo Serina + Greg B. Macabenta + Irineo P. Goce or KaPule2 + Percival Cruz + Juan DelaCruz or Textmani + Demosthenes B. Donato. + + **Writings 9 Book, April 2011,** Articles by Judge Simeon dumdum Jr + Gemma Cruz Araneta + Larry Henares Jr + Tony Joaquin + Allen Gaborro + Atty. Toto Causing + Mar-Vic Cagurangn + Emily Espanol Derry, Poet + Elyn Jean Felarca, Poet + Naysan A. Albaytar + Laura Wade, Blogger + Perter Allan Mariano + Marge Trajeco-Aberasturi + Julia Carreon Lagoc + Irineo P. Goce or KaPulle2 + Anonymous. + +

**Writings 10 Book, July, 2010,** Articles by Atty.Ted Lagutan + Percival C. Cruz + Allen Gaborro + Peter Allan Mariano + M.L. Munoz + Alvib T. Tabaniag + Resty Odon + Dr. Phili S. Chua + Dr. Cesar D. Candari

# A JOURNEY UNTO PEACE

+ Anonymous. + + **Writings 11 Book, August, 2011** +
1, SONA In English and Filipino, by President Benigno
Aquino III (P-Noy) + 2, Telltale Signs: SONA and the
Dogfight Over Spratlys, by Rodel Rodis + Atty. Ted
Laguatan + Tatay Jobo Elizes + Jeremiah M. Opiniano
+ OFW Journalists + Bob & Carol Hammerslag +
Roger P. Olivares + Rob Ceralvo + Anonymous +
Irineo P. Goce or KaPule2 + Random. + +

**Writings 12 Book, April 2012** + Articles By Orion
Perez Dumdum + Julia C. Lagoc + Honorio M. Cruz,
MD + Ben Gonzales, MD + Mar-Vic Cagurangan +
Marisa Lerias + Gerry Partido + Dr. Cesar D. Candari +
Erwin De Leon + Jovelyn B. Revilla + Tatay Jobo
Elizes + + **Writings 13 Book, July 2012** + Articles by
Raymundo E. Narag + M.L. Munoz + Sonia Barbara gl
Munoz + Pamela Joy Agtoto + Percival C. Cruz + Tatay
Jobo Elizes + Jhakie Eslit Bayobay + Reygel Saplad
Perales. + + **Timely Writings 14, 2013** + Articles by
Cesar F. Lumba + Eugenio Pulmano + Late Jesse
Robredo + Antonio Nievera + Alvin T. Tabaniag +
Kevin L. Nadal + Anonymous + Fred Natividad +
Anonymous + Ellen Tordesillas + Lat Capt. Rene N.
Jarque + +

**Timeless Writings-15 (TW15), 2014** + Articles by SC
Justice Antonio T. Carpio + Atty Dodel Rodis + Atty.
Ted Laguatan + Sona by Pres. Benigno Aquino III + F.
Sionil Jose + Dr. Philipi Stack + Racz Kelly, Padilla +
Bert Armada.+ + **Timeless Writings-16 (TW16), 2014** +
Articles about The Martyrs of Camarines Norte + by
Rodel Rodis + R.A.Gubalane + Robert Bernardo +
Pres. Aquino's SONA 2014 + + **Timeless Writings-17
(TW17), 2014** + Articles by Rodel Rodis+ Jose P.

# A JOURNEY UNTO PEACE

Rizal+ Irineo Goce+ Julia Lagos + Alvin Tabaniag+ Ragubalane + Red Butterfly+ Cesar Torres + + Timeless Writings-18 (TW18) + Articles by Rodel Rodis + Raul Manglapus + Ragubalane + Allen Gaborro + Manuel Vergara + +

Solo Authored Books: + + +

Book A, Turning Points, *Job Elizes Sr,1968 (Reissue 2009)* + + + Book B, Be Considerate For Once, *Tatay Jobo Elizes (Jr), 2013* Book C, Piglets Unlimited - Wealth, *Tatay Jobo Elizes, 2009* + + + Book D, Out of the Misty Sea We Must, *Cesar Lumba, 2010* + + + Book E, Fulfilled – *Gonzales Reynaldo, Editor, 2010* + + +

Book F - Reflections - *Bert Guiang, 2010* + + + Book G, Writings 7 - My Vintage Pics, *Tatay Jobo Elizes, 2010* + Book H, May Bagwis Ang Pag-ibig, *Percival C. Cruz* + + + Book I, Letters To Matrimony, *Irineo P. Goce, Ka Pule2, 2011* + Book J, Songs I Wish You Knew, *Soledad R. Juan, 2011* + + +

Book K, Make My Day, *Larry Henares Jr., 1993, Re-issue 2011* + Book L, Our Guerrero Family, *Tatay Jobo Elizes, 2010* + + + Book M, Handy Jokes, *Tatay J. Elizes, 2011* + Book N, FaveArt 1, *Tatay Jobo Elizes, 2011* + + Book O, Beyond idle thoughts, *MLMunoz, Sept,2011* + + +

Book P, Cracks In The Armor, *Mariano Ngan, Oct 2011* + + + Book Q, FaveArt 2, *Tatay Jobo Elizes, 2011* + + Book R, Balitang Kutsero, *Perry Diaz, Jan*

# A JOURNEY UNTO PEACE

2012 + + + Book S, FaveArt3, *Tatay Jobo, 2011* + + +
Book T, FaveArt4 *,2012, Tatay Jobo* + + +

Book U, Stack Family Journals, *Phil & Fe Stack,
2012* + + + Book V, Emily, An Adoption Journey,
*Romerl Elizes, 2012* + + + Book W, Hermes Alegre Art
Gallery, *TJ & Hermes, 2012* + + + Book X, Masaya Din,
Malungkot Din, *Jovelyn B. Revilla, 2012* Book Y, Tiis,
Sipag At Tiyaga, *Raquel Delfin Padilla, 2012* + + +
Book Z, Until I Meet You, *Jhackie Eslit Bayobay, 2012*
+ + +

Book AA, Buhay At Pag-ibig, *Argel Lucero Tamayo,
2012* + + + Book AB, Hail to the Second Best, *Dr.
Philip Stack, 2012* + + + Book AC, Life Bus, *Mommy
Joyce Pineda-Faulmino, 2012* + + + Book AD, My
Candid Musings, *Monette Dioquino Calugay, 2012* +
Book AE, Tickets to Life, *Maria Lourdes Jesalva,
2012* + + +

Book AF, The Dove Files, *Mike Portes, 2012* + + +
Book AG, Nursing Vignettes, *Jocelyn Cerrudo Sese,
2012* + Book AH, Poor Ba Us, *R.A. Gubalane, 2012* + +
+ Book AI, Summer Idyll, *Avelina Gil, 2012* + + Book
AJ, Legacy (Pamana), *Rachel Astrero, 2012* + + Book
AK, Narratives Old & New, *Avelina J. Gil, 2013* + +

Book AL, Buhay Saudi, *Adele J. Esic, 2013* + + Book
AM, Buhay Ofw Atbp, *Jessica Napat, 2013* + + Book
AN, Mga Tula Ng Buhay, *Angelita C. Esguerra, 2013* +
+ Book AO, Not by Bread Alone, *Judge Lily V.
Magtolis, 2013* + + Book AP, Jokes Collection-2, *Tatay
Jobo Elizes, 2013* + + +

# A JOURNEY UNTO PEACE

Book AR, *My Writings Sometimes, Tatay Jobo Elizes,* 2013 + + Book AS, Sa 'Yo Na Ako, *Shayne A. Martinez, 2013* + + Book AT, My Kin's Family Trees, *Tatay Jobo Elizes, 2013* + + Book AU, Rizal Family Tree & Others, *Tatay Jobo Elizes, 2013* + + Book AV, Make My Day-2, Nice & Nasty, *L. Henares, 2013 (1993)* + +

Book AW, Make My Day-3, Cecilia, Love, *L.Henares, 2013 (1993)*Book AX, Handy Lyrics-1, *Tatay Jobo Elizes, 2013* + + Book AY, Ang Biblos, *Rev. Dr. Eugenio Guerrero, 2014 (1929)* + + Book AZ, Make My Day-4, *Sweet & Sour, L. Henares, 2014 (1993)* + +

Book BA, Life's Journey, True Stories, *Dr. Phil Stack, 2014* + + Book BB, Gerry Gil Writings, 2014, Danny Gil + + Book BC, Mr. President, *Hermie Rotea, 2014* + + Book BD, Nostalgic Pics *1, Tatay Jobo Elizes, 2014* + + Book BE, MakeMyDay-5, Saints & Sinners, *Henares, 2014 (1993)* + +

Book BF, MakeMyDay-6, Villains & Heroes, *Henares, 2014 (1993)* + + Book BG, Nostalgic Pics 2 (ElizesClan), *TatayJE, 2014* + + Book BH, MakeMyDay-7, Tough & Tender, *Henares, 2014(1993)* + + Book BI, MakeMyDay-8, Light & Shadow, *Henares, 2014(1993)* + + Book BJ, MakeMyDay-9, Give & Take, *Henares, 2014(1993)* + + Book BK, MakeMyDay-10, ToBeOrNotToBe, *Henares, 2014(1993)* +

Book BL,Emily Forever In Love, Poems,*Emily Espanol Derry, 2013* + + Book BM, The Sinatra Songbook, *Henares, 2014* + + Book BN, The Gaborro Reader, *Allen Gaborro, 2010* + + Book BO, Ramon H.

# A JOURNEY UNTO PEACE

Lopez - *Art Gallery, 2014* + + *Book BP,* Philippines Via Old Pics-1, *Tatay Jobo, 2014* + +

Book BQ, Ronna Manansala - *Art Gallery, 2014* + + Book BR, **Philippines Via Old Pics-2,** *Tatay Jobo, 2014* + + *Book BS,* **Being Good-A Medley Of Love,** *Dr. Phil Stack, 2014* + + Book BT, **Lifestream Fisherman, A Filipino Odyssey,** *Paul Dalde, Jul2014* + + **Book BU, Kristina Reed Manansala, Art Gallery-1**, *August 2014.*+ +

Book BV, **Hermes Art Gallery-2**, *Sep2014,* + + Book BW, **Fave Art-5**, *Tatay Jobo, Sep2014* + + Book BX, **Cash & Credits, Make My Day-11**, *Larry Henares, Sept 2014* + + **Book BY, Rise & Fall, Make My Day-12,** *Larry Henares, Oct 2014* + + Book BZ, **Swans & Swine, Make My Day-13,** *Larry Henares, Oct 2014* + +

Book CA, **Touch & Go, Make My Day-14,** *Larry Henares, Oct 2014* + + Book CB, **Life & Death, Make My Day-15**, *Larry Henares, Oct2014* + + Book CC, **Kiss & Bite, Make My day -16**, *Larry Henares, Oct 2014* + + Book CD, **Good & Evil, Make My Day-17,** *Larry Henares, Oct2014* + + Book CE, **Beast & Beauty, Make My Day-18**, *Larry Henares, 2014* + +

Book CF, **Beggar & King, Make My Day-19,** *Larry Henares, Oct 2014* + + Book CG, **Trash & Treasures, Make My Day-20,** *Larry Henares, Oct 2014* + + Book CH, **Wear & Tear, Make My Day-21**, *Larry Henares, Oct 2014* + + Book CI, **Why Blame the President,** *Irineo P. Goce, Oct 2014* + + Book CJ, **Angel & Devil, Make My Day-22**, *Larry Henares, Oct 2014* + +

# A JOURNEY UNTO PEACE

Book CK, Pretty Ugly, Make My Day-23, *Larry Henares, Oct 2014* + + Book CL, Salvation & Damnation, Make My Day-24, *Larry Henares, Oct 2014* + + Book CM, Don Daniel Maramba, *Larry Henarez & Edith Perez de Tagle, Oct 2014* + + Book CN, Hilarion G. Henares, *Larry Henares & Edith Perez de Tagle, Oct 2014* + +Book CO, FaveArt-5 ++

Book CP, FaveArt-6, Book CQ, FaveArt-7, Book CR, FaveArt-8 (all Fave Art books *by TatayJobo), 2014* ++ Book CS, Minsan May Isang Puta, *Mike Portes, 2014* + + Book CT, Ramblings A, *Danny Gil, 2014* + + Book CU, Ramblings-B, *Danny Gil, 2014* + + Book CV, Grace Esmeralda Album, *by her, 2014* + + Book CW, Secrets of a Romantic Man, *Dr. Phil Stack, 2014* + + Book CX, Ramblings-C, *Danny Gil, 2014* + + Book CY, Ramblings-D, *Danny Gil, 2014* + + Book CZ, Ramblings-E, *Danny Gil, 2014* ++ Book DA, Tenacious Nurse-1, *Gretheline Bolandrina, 2014* + + Book DB, Tenacious Nurse-2, *Gretheline Ramos-Bolandrina, 2015* + + Book DC, Of Words I Have Found, *Dan Jimenez (danmeljim), 2015* + +

Book DD, Tanjay East Coast Magazine, Issue 1, *Feb 2015* + + Book DE, Tanjay East Coast Magazine, Issue 2, *April 2015* + + Book DF, Catechism Manual, *Dr. Latorre, April 2015* + + *Book DG,* Tanjay East Coast Magazine, Extra Issue 2A, *April 2015* + + *Book DH, Wedding Album, Anita & Barry, May 2015* + + *Book DI, Tanjay E. Coast Magazine, Poconos, May 2015* + + *Book DJ, Baptism Guidebook, Dr. Latorre, May 2015* + + *Book DK, Chita, a Memoir, Tony Joaquin* + + *Book DL, A Journey Unto Peace, Dr. Phil Stack, June2015*+ +

Permission had been granted by the author/authors to print their books  under my free self-publishing service. They own copyrights to their works.

**_Tatay Jobo Elizes_**